An Epistle on Expectation

Titles in the Series
Letters to the Devoted Follower of Christ

(in the order in which they were written)

AN EPISTLE

ON

EXPECTATION

By

An Anchorite of the Church

Scriptures quoted from the King James Version (KJV) of the Bible. Please note that pronouns referring to God have been capitalized, though they are not in the KJV Bible.

ISBN-13: 979-8-3305-4165-2

Please note that this writer possesses no affiliation with any particular religious order or denomination of the Christian Church, including Catholic or Anglican or any other denomination that might be associated with the formal office of anchorite. There can be a difference between fulfilling the religious rules of an office to pursuing a personal & layperson calling for the sake of the Church.

An Epistle

on Expectation

My dear friend in Christ, as my letter on the sub-
ject of expectation, I wish to send you a copy of a
little story that, though old, treats in a memorable
way how the believer covenanted to a loving God
ought to view His care of His own. It was written
by Emily Steele Elliott circa 1897. Perhaps you
are familiar with it. Regardless, I urge you to read
it again. We need to read and reread God's good
words to us, to deeply embed them in our hearts
so that in times of spiritual aridity, they are a

fount of living water for our thirst.* This story is a good way to get some scriptures into your soul, as you will easily see as you read it. I hope it helps you as it has helped me.

Just a note: the original story did not include the references for the scriptures quoted, so I have included them for you here in footnotes.

The peace of God be with you always,

Your friend in Christ

* John 7:37-38

EXPECTATION CORNER

OR

"IS YOUR DOOR OPEN?"

Emily Steele Elliott
c. 1897

It was New Year's Eve. Distant bells rang out mingled Christmas and New Year's messages to a joyous rhythm of their own; and, as from the great city came up in deep undertone a continuous roar of human life and occupation, I wondered as to the homes, rich and poor—as to the hearts, outwardly severed though truly united—in which those messages would meet with a responsive echo.

Then my eye fell on the Book before me; and the words on which it lighted seemed to sound out an answering Christmas chime, which had there taken form and shape, *"Truly my soul waiteth upon God: from Him cometh my salvation!"* [*]

> *"For unto us a Child is born!*
> *For unto us a Son is given!"* [†]

rang the bells.

"FROM HIM COMETH MY SALVATION!" rang out again from the Psalm-book; *"He only is my Rock and my Salvation!"* [‡] "All my salvation and all my desire!"[§] In the quietness of a solitary room, to which times and seasons bring little outer change, chimes of Heaven often linger and repeat themselves, as is only possible in the stilled atmosphere from which earth's louder voices are shut out.

And, as the twilight fell, it seemed to me that, all at once, the bells sounded forth

---

[*] Psalm 62:1

[†] Isaiah 9:6

[‡] Psalm 62:2

[§] II Samuel 23:5

other words through the frosty air—words as of bugle-call for the coming year:

> *"Now wait thou only upon God!*
> *My expectation is from Him!"* *

and a bright flicker from the fire wakened up the same message from the old hereditary Psalm of royal melody, so that it stood out almost with the vividness of a new inscription.

"MY EXPECTATION IS FROM HIM!"

Is it? And for what? And for how much? The thought would not be dismissed— rather, was bidden to remain.

How much am I expecting? How much do I know of waiting upon God? Should I be very much surprised if all my desires were visibly, actually to be fulfilled now?

Then came thoughts of humiliation— thoughts of contrition. So much promised! So little expected! So much chartered! So little claimed! So much praying! So little watching! No: so *little* praying? So little conscious receiving!

---

* Psalm 62:5

Ah! it all was too true; and on and on rang the notes in clear octave of harmony,

> *"My soul, wait only upon God:*
> *My expectation is from Him!"*

Then, after a while, my thoughts wandered to a seaside parish belonging to the history of other days, and to one home and another inhabited by those who had learned secrets of communication with Heaven concerning which many of us seemed but poor scholars. And, as other memories intertwined themselves with these of sacred association, portraits from the past and present stood forth in the gloom with almost lifelike vividness, and, in half-allegory, shaped themselves into the history here, as for old cottage friends, set forth in homely words, which history may be called:

"A CHRONICLE OF THE REDEEMED LAND."

It ran thus:

Adam Slowman lived in a cottage on the Redeemed Land, which was a portion of an estate so large that—go which way you would—you could not see beyond it. The

Owner of this land was honored far and near; and, on the particular part of the property to which Adam belonged, He was most especially loved and obeyed. The reason why it was called the Redeemed Land was that, after a rebellion a long time before, which had brought the people to what looked like hopeless ruin, His own Son had, by actually coming and living like a poor cottager amongst them, and toiling as one of them, worked out a plan for their being taken once more into favor, by paying in His own person the fine which had been laid on them as a forfeit for their evil doings.

So, ever after, all whose names were down in the petition which was sent up to the Lord of the estate asking forgiveness for the past, and claiming right to a part in the payment worked out by His Son, who had made Himself their Brother in sorrow and trouble, received special promises of love and favor. To each one a lease or covenant was given, by which he held his house and ground—a lease promising him many and various rights and grants for himself and his family—with the assurance that, although at some time, sooner or later, he might have to give them up, he should have a far better and more lasting home in a glorious province of his Lord's kingdom—nay, in the glories of His own out-stretching palace—when home and hearth should fail here.

If I were to tell you half the good things of this Redeemed Land, you would be surprised at the love and kindness with which it was cared for by the Owner. Though around it much of the estate lay waste, every house there had its claim to a supply of the purest water, specially, and with boundless care, brought over the hills for its inhabitants. Then there were fair meadows and quiet woods, to which each one had a pass-key and right of admission; and there were orchards with rich fruit to be had for the asking, and all manner of other privileges, by the covenant of each house placed within reach of the humblest cottager, which mention of tenant rights brings me back to my story of Adam Slowman.

He was getting on in life, was Adam, and he had for a long time been settled in his house on the Redeemed Land, which, if you look carefully in the map of the property, is written down there as the *"Land of Forgiveness of Sin."* But he was a slow scholar, and used to grumble that his sight wasn't so good as it might be in looking up his covenant, which all the same he held to firm and fast, as his one security for the promises on which he counted.

Adam lived poor, so to speak, when he might have lived rich. His windows were dull and clouded, when, if only he had rubbed away the cobwebs and dust which darkened them, a glad sunshine would always have brightened every room in the cottage. He complained of a want of fresh water; but, as his next-door neighbor often reminded him, he had only to see that his own pipe, connecting his place with the living fountain from the hills, was kept clear and open, to have enough and over without stint or hindrance.

Then he used sometimes to bemoan himself that food was scarce. "Why man," said his next-door neighbor, Widow Fulljoy, when she heard this, "you're bringing up words in saying that which seem like accusing our lordly Master of keeping His tenants half-starved! Isn't His own granary, where food enough is stored for generations to come, right there in sight of our windows, and all you need bought and paid for, that you might have it free? You must know as well as I do that you've only to give in a petition, and get it rightly signed, and wait for the answers, to have day by day enough, not only to keep you from starving, but, what's more, to make your countenance appear fatter and fresher than that of the children of any other king!"

"Ah, neighbor," Adam would reply, in a voice as dreary as the wind in winter, "you're right, I often do believe! But you seem to get hold of things which I can't. That oil of joy for mourning,[*] found to you year by year, is what I don't see how I'm ever to come in for. I don't think it's down in my covenant; no, nor clothes like yours. That garment of praise for the spirit of heaviness,[†] which our visitor said the other day was the livery we are expected to wear

---

[*] Isaiah 61:3
[†] Isaiah 61:3

all down this way—it's a deal richer clothing than, it seems to me, I've got a right to put on, poor and worthless as I am. I *do* thank Him in my poor way for all He's done for me, but—but—"

"But you think it's humbler to tune '*O come let us sing unto the Lord; let us heartily rejoice in the strength of our salvation!*' * to the Dead March in the Lamentations," put in Widow Fulljoy, with energy, "or to sound it out, or, what's nearer the truth, sorrow it out, as if it was somebody else's praising you'd got to do by mistake, having no right to a thanksgiving of your own! Why, man, people had best put on black crape over their helmets of salvation† to show their humility in that sort of praising, instead of looking right up to the One who's saved them with, 'He loved me and gave Himself for me,' ‡ in their song."

"Now, I *do* think you're a bit too strong there, neighbor," said poor Adam, meekly; "if you was as poor as I am, you'd know

---

* Psalm 95:1—as rendered in the Psalter in *The Book of Common Prayer.*

† Ephesians 6:17

‡ E.g., Ephesians 5:2

how hard it is to sound out one's thanks like that. I wouldn't be the one to bring a discredit on my dear Lord, no not for all the world; but, you see, we're different. We're the same family, I know, but—but—you're a richer branch. Yes—there it is!" repeated Adam, as if he had got hold of a new light with a ray of comfort in it; "I feel as if I was a sort of poor relation to you, and couldn't ever hope for all that's granted to those with stronger faith."

" 'Poor relation,' man! and pray what call have you to be poor, with bank-notes there hidden away between the leaves of your Covenant-book, which are never so much as taken out and presented? I do declare," she said, half to herself, "he's like that poor crazy nobleman down in the shires that was richer than a prince, and had got the notion into his head that he was nigh on bankrupt, and half-starved himself and his family as well, and died after years of leading the life of a pauper.

"Dear old friend," she continued, gently; "*do* think that it's hard on a rich Father—loving as He's rich—when His children go so poorly clad and complaining of scarcity.

But I see how it is: you're weak, and you're getting on in years, and you feel as if it was too much for your head to be thinking out a deal of what's told us in our covenant of our Lord's plans of providing for His own. So it seems to me what you've got to do is to ask Him to do the *remembering* for you as well as the giving: that's it," she nodded to herself—"the remembering and the giving both—the seeing what you want and the making it good out of His great love and riches. I know for certain, neighbor, if only you send in a petition like that to His great house, He'll see to it directly and answer it."

"But how shall I put it into words, neighbor?" said Adam. "Somehow my petitions only seem to get to Him now and then; you're a deal a better scholar than I, now that I'm old and a bit dim of sight and slow of understanding."

"Well, it seems to me there are words ready found for us," answered Widow Fulljoy, going to a cupboard in which Adam's Covenant-book was carefully kept. "Here are some—

" 'Lord, I am oppressed; undertake for me! *
Plead Thou the causes of my soul! †
Arise, O Lord, plead Thine own cause! ‡
Be surety unto Thy servant for good.' §

" 'Show me Thy ways, O Lord: teach me
Thy paths. Lead me in Thy truth, and teach me:
for Thou art the God of my salvation: on Thee
do I wait all the day. Remember, O Lord, Thy
tender mercies and Thy lovingkindnesses; for
they have been ever of old. Remember not the
sins of my youth, nor my transgressions: accord-
ing to Thy mercy, remember Thou me, for Thy
goodness' sake, O Lord!' **

"Send in those words, Adam, and see
what they will bring you. Here you must
add: *'This petition comes from my Lord's hum-*
ble servant, who is waiting with open door his
Lord's answer.' "

"If only He will deign to read it and
send an answer!" sighed Adam, doubtfully.

---

[*] Isaiah 38:14

[†] Lamentations 3:58

[‡] Psalm 74:22

[§] Psalm 119:122

[**] Psalm 25:4-7

"If only!" echoed Widow Fulljoy, with a sort of receipt in advance in her tone. "Why, neighbor, one would think you lived in the land of condemnation instead of the Land of Forgiveness of Sin! 'a land of hills and valleys, and which drinketh water of the rain of heaven: a land which our Lord careth for: the eyes of our Lord always upon it, from the beginning of the year even unto the end of the year.' * *If only!* I know how it was with me when I sent in that very same petition, long ago, and how, with all sorts of blessed incomings, I got back this note with the post-mark from my Lord's own palace—'Good and upright is the Lord: therefore will He teach sinners in the way. The meek will He guide in judgment; and the meek will He teach His way. All the paths of the Lord are mercy and truth unto such as keep His covenant and His testimonies.' † Oh, it *was* brave to get a token like that," she added, "and all as true as the sunlight."

---

* Deuteronomy 11:11-12

† Psalm 25:8-10

"At all events I shall hope something may come of it," answered Adam. "I don't want to seem ungrateful, neighbor," he still murmured, "but often and often, when I *have* sent a petition, and really from my heart, it hasn't seemed to make much difference."

"I wonder whether you've seen to the terms of our Covenant-book," was the reply. "The sending in the petition isn't all. There are three parts to that blessed trade with the palace of our Lord. Look here, it says, 'CONTINUE *in prayer*,' then 'WATCH *in the same* *'; and then, when you've watched—and when did He ever tell you to watch in vain?—*then*," continued Widow Fulljoy, triumphantly, "then the *thanksgiving*. Ah! that thanksgiving! it's like all one's life-joy worked up into a psalm."

It was with a half-sigh of relief that Adam signed his name to his petition. After he had written it down, and put it into the post-office set up beside his door by the Lord of the estate, he seemed ever so much lighter while his old friend showed him in

---

* Colossians 4:2

his own book a record of how that same Lord had cared for His people long ago, when they were cast down and too low to take hold of the promises which were there waiting for them to claim.

"It's written out here," she said, "where it's told how they were minished and brought low." *

"Like me!" put in Adam.

"And they couldn't bring to mind all that He was ready to give them—too dull, so to speak, to read, and too short of memory to remember, and too low down almost to hope. And see here what it says, man: *'He remembered* FOR THEM *this cove-nant!'*† Ah, that's what I was saying! He did the remembering as well as the giving. He pleaded with Himself, so to speak, for what He knew was promised in His own mind for them; and He gave it them, not because they were clever in asking, but because He read in His own word loads and loads of meaning which they couldn't understand,

---

* Psalm 107:39
† Exodus 2:24

15

but which for His own sake He wanted to make good to them.

"Why, there's rights and privileges in our covenants, Adam, which are as much greater than anything we can understand as are the very descriptions of Heaven itself. It came to me long ago how my Lord would be honored in my getting hold of more of His riches, and living out more like a king's daughter, and having her place according, and a song of His goodness always telling of a full store. And I thought how much more there was in His promises than I could even call to mind; and so, as I put Him in remembrance of one and another, I said, in my petition, 'But oh, my Lord, there's more in that than I can think or tell, but Thou knowest Thine own mind to give, and Thine own riches in glory; so do Thou *remember for me* Thy covenant, and send the answer accordingly, and Thy servant's door will be open for Thy gifts, and my heart expecting and my eyes waiting for Thy coming!' And I got such a store, and am always getting more, that I've learnt to see He means what He says.

And so do you the same, Adam; and then—
what's more—thank Him!"

And as Widow Fulljoy went out into
the sunshine, and turned into her own little
house, where a wealth of peace and treasures of hope and comfort all round told of
a bounteous Giver, Adam heard her favorite song, ringing out through the stillness:

> When long ago I took Thee at Thy word,
>   My sins were washed away;
> Now for all else I claim Thy promise, Lord,
>   As mine for every day!
>
> Be mine the stream from everlasting hills—
>   Thy Spirit's boundless grace;
> Be mine the peace which lowliest temple fills
>   Where Thou hast dwelling-place.
>
> Be mine with rich provision to show forth
>   The bounty of my King!
> Full stores of grace should tell His boundless
>   worth
>   Whose royal love I sing.
>
> Oh! for receiving that shall glorify
>   The Lord whom I implore!
> My listening soul entreats Him to draw nigh,
>   And waits with open door. *

---

* Elliott was also a hymn writer and poet.

~

Adam had not long to wait after sending in his petition to the Great House. Through his open door a Messenger came all silently to his side, with words of blessing and peace.

"You called for me in your petition, and wrote, 'Show me Thy ways, and teach me Thy paths!' so I have come, Adam," he said; "but your house is dark, and your place is scantily furnished, and you seem starved and poorly clothed, instead of living like the King's own."

Adam looked sad and ashamed. "It's all true, my Lord," he said. "I seem too low down to help myself, and too unworthy to get hold of better things, though I love my Kingly Master, and *do* praise Him for putting me in this Redeemed Land, and for so frankly forgiving all my debt, and letting me look up to Him as my Friend and Sovereign Ruler."

The Visitor looked pityingly and yet sadly upon him, and then went to the window and breathed upon it. And in a little the sunlight streamed in right upon Adam, and lit up the page where his Covenant-book lay open, and fell upon the words, "ALL THINGS ARE YOURS," * so that they stood out in new fresh light to his eyes, while, from Widow Fulljoy's cottage, a scrap of a hymn, which she was singing as she stood at her door, was borne on the wind. The words sounded out—

> Thy blessed unction from above
> Is comfort, life, and fire of love;
> Enable with perpetual light
> The dullness of our blinded sight! †

Then the Visitor looked to where a scanty supply of clouded water told part of the reason of Adam's being weak and low; and, going to where the connection lay for a supply from the hill fountains, he cleared out so much rubbish from the pipe that you would have wondered how any one could have got enough to live on, let alone thriving. Then, when the clear stream, with life and healing in every drop, began to flow in,

---

* I Corinthians 3:21-23

† The Hymn "Veni, Creator Spiritus" in *The Book of Common Prayer*, though the hymn itself seems to date back to the ninth century.

and Adam's Visitor brought him a full draught, you wouldn't have known him for the same man! There came such a light to his eyes, and such a firmness to his limbs, which had been trembling like one in the palsy, that already you could see that he was being nourished from the King's country.

Then the Visitor looked at the cupboard and found a few bits of bread which had lain there some time, good and pure bread, indeed, but so scanty, and left so long, that the question came once more as to how Adam had been getting on at all.

"Stale manna isn't our Lord's plan for His tenants," he said; "new corn of the land is what He has for His people—the bread from His own palace. It seems to me, Adam, that it is long since you had yours fresh. Why, even in the rebellious provinces, it is told abroad how 'the Lord hath visited His people in giving them bread.'" *

"It's all true, my Lord," was the answer, and Adam looked with something of shame at his shelves: "but—but—I fall back upon

---

* Ruth 1:6

what I keep there, and am thankful not to be quite starved."

"Quite starved, man!" was the reply, "quite starved! and you living on the Redeemed Land, and the store wagons coming past your door each day with 'MERCIES NEW EVERY MORNING' * written up in large letters on them, and the parcels ready to give in for each one who has the receipt ready—'GREAT IS THY FAITHFUL- NESS!' † *Starved!* When the fruits are there from the Lord's own gardens—provisions from His own house! Starved! When there's such planning, and care, and fore- thought put into making up every supply for each one of His tenants every day, that to undo it and take out these new mercies that are sent, and hold them up to the light, and see them unfolding, and mark them fit- ting into every need that comes through all the hours, makes the whole day like a gift- day, which it is, and its song, 'Whoso is wise and will observe these things, even he

---

* Lamentations 3:22-23

† Lamentations 3:23

shall understand the lovingkindness of the Lord!' *

"But what's been the matter, Adam, has been that *your door has been shut,* or only half open now and then. The stores have been there for you, but there's been no one looking out to take them in day by day. Every now and then, indeed, just a little chink has been unfastened—enough for a bit of bread here and a stray fruit there, but little more than starvation allowance; and you bringing discredit on your royal Lord by little expecting and little receiving.

"Then your petitions, Adam, have had so many '*ifs*' and '*buts*'—there have come along with them so many '*I don't expects*' and '*perhaps,*' and so many '*I don't know whether this'll ever get into my Lord's hands, and, if it does, I don't know whether He'll hear me,*' that they have been—though you may not have meant them so—half insults to His goodness. As if He had paid such a price for setting up His royal posts that there should be a doubt as to His receiving and seeing to any petition sent out to Him

---

* Psalm 107:43

in due course, and according to His orders, and made in His Son's name!"

"I never meant—I don't think I ever put such words into my petitions," faltered Adam; "I know they were often badly written, for I'm a poor scholar—but—but—"

"Scholar, man! There are thousands and thousands of letters which go straight into His Dead Letter Office which are all made up of dictionary words, and of what people outside call fine scholarship. No! 'Remember Thy word unto Thy servant upon which Thou hast caused me to hope!' * has the scholarship in it which brings in the answer. 'God be merciful to me a sinner!'† which, for His Son's sake, long ago procured for you the free pardon and the place on this property—every one in the House giving way before that petition—had no fine words sent in with it. Humility and confession of sin are the first lessons which are taught in your Lord's own school, set up for those whom He would have on His

---

* Psalm 119:49
† Luke 18:13

estate; and humility and trust on-and-on are the next. Look to your Covenant-book, Adam, for it seems to me you've stopped low down in the classes, and see what scholarship is needed for the petitions that get in and are heard by Him. *'This poor man cried, and the Lord heard him and delivered him out of all his troubles.'* * *'For the oppression of the poor, for the sighing of the needy, now will I arise, saith the Lord!'* † There's the scholarship—the cry and the sighs—then the watching and the praise.

"Why, you know, Adam, that your Lord's own Son, who paid such a price to free you, and get you a place on the estate, makes it His business to sign every petition sent in in His name. And look how He is longing to give each one what is best and needful for him! He left these words for all who should seek pardon through Him, the very last night of His being down here, to work out by His own suffering a right to His Father's love and gifts of blessing: 'Verily, verily, I say unto you, Whatsoever

---

* Psalm 34:6
† Psalm 12:5

ye shall ask the Father in My Name, He will give it you. Hitherto have ye asked nothing in My Name: ask, and ye shall receive, that your joy may be full.' * That's what you may call a fine bank-note for one on the Royal Estate; but remember that, when you're sending in a petition, every '*if*' and '*but*,' and '*It's pretty much a chance if I'm heard!*' and '*I don't feel as if my prayer would get much higher than the ceiling!*' and '*I don't think I'm likely to have an answer!*' come out as a great blot, and sometimes covers up the writing, so that it scarcely gets read.

"There are no ifs and buts about those words in your Covenant-book: 'The Lord upholdeth all that fall, and raiseth up all those that be bowed down. The eyes of all wait upon Thee: and Thou givest them their meat in due season. Thou openest Thine hand, and satisfiest the desire of every living thing. The Lord is righteous in all His ways, and holy in all His works. The Lord is nigh unto all them that call upon Him, to all that call upon Him in truth. He will fulfil the desire of them that

---

* John 16:23-24

fear Him; He also will hear their cry, and will save them.' * That's the way the supplies come in for those who see to it that there's nothing between them and their receiving from the royal storehouse. '*My soul, wait thou only upon God, for my expectation is from Him!*'† There, Adam, put down in plain figures how much you've *expected* from Him, and you'll see why you've gone on in this shabby half-alive fashion! Now come with me!"

And very swiftly Adam found himself carried away to a part of the estate of which he had, indeed, heard, but which he had never expected to see. A long range of storehouses met his eye, from which heavily-laden wagons were going forth to all parts of the property, bringing out supplies, sometimes exactly according to the petitions sent in from the tenants themselves, which were kept in a book for reference, and often in stores and gifts, which the Lord of the property, who knew everything about each one, saw to be better

---

* Psalm 145:14-19

† Psalm 62:5

suited for them than the very things they asked for. Over these storehouses was written in large letters—

"THE LORD OVER ALL IS RICH UNTO ALL THAT CALL UPON HIM." [*]

And underneath—

"*The expectation of the poor shall not perish.*" [†]

But from these Adam's Guide turned away to a huge outbuilding some distance off in the shade, and said, "Do you know what this is, Adam?"

"No, my Lord," was the answer.

"This," said the Messenger, "is the 'MISSED BLESSINGS OFFICE.' Here are kept stores and gifts which were all ready to be sent forth for many, who, for one cause or another, never received them, one common reason being that the door was closed when the store-chariots came round. That door of expectation—though you would hardly believe it—many keep shut, even when they have sent in a request for the very thing which is supplied for their

---

[*] Romans 10:12
[†] Psalm 9:18

need, and though they write in their petition, '*On Thee do I wait all the day.*' " [*]

Adam looked shy and uneasy at these words, and still more so when his Guide opened the gate of the outer court, and led him through the large halls. Such numbers of parcels, all with the date of their sending out, and, alas! each one telling of its having missed an owner.

Over one department of these stores, where quantities of raw material lay massed, was written up, "YE HAVE NOT BECAUSE YE ASK NOT." [†]

Over a second, "YOUR SINS HAVE WITHHOLDEN GOOD THINGS FROM YOU." [‡]

Over a third, "THEY LIMITED THE HOLY ONE OF ISRAEL." [§] "LET NOT THAT MAN THAT DOUBTETH THINK THAT HE SHALL RECEIVE ANYTHING OF THE LORD" [**]; and just underneath was a handbill, with the words, "*Doors found closed, and no entrance for chartered gifts.*"

---

[*] Psalm 25:5
[†] James 4:2
[‡] Jeremiah 5:25
[§] Psalm 78:41
[**] James 1:7

Over another was the inscription, "CONDITIONS UNFULFILLED"; and a placard underneath bore the notice:

"If ye abide in Me, and My words abide in you,
ye shall ask what ye will,
and it shall be done unto you.[*]
Bring ye all the tithes into the storehouse,
that there may be meat in Mine house,
and PROVE ME NOW *herewith,*
saith the Lord of hosts,
if I will not open you the windows of heaven,
and pour you out a blessing,
that there shall not be
room enough to receive it." [†]

Over one darkly and distantly seen store was written: "FORFEITED BLESSINGS"; and underneath, *"Ye ask and receive not because ye ask amiss, that ye may consume it upon your lusts."* [‡]

Meanwhile Adam's face grew more and more downcast, as he saw the riches, the royal provisions, the packages prepared

---

[*] John 15:7

[†] Malachi 3:10

[‡] James 4:3

with bounteous care, which would have made thousands rich and happy, lying neglected. But he had yet more to learn. His Guide led him quickly into the third of the chambers, which opened out into a large court, and there, ranged in order, were what seemed endless parcels, all sorted on shelves with the names written above them of those for whom they had been sent out, and who had yet never received them.

Before one range of shelves the Messenger stopped. The name written up over these was "*Adam Slowman.*" Adam gazed in mute surprise. Those crowded shelves! The very things stored closely together for which he had wished, and had now and then asked, with many a blot, however, on his petition; treasures which, though they were there for him, he had not received.

"I thought the line was blocked often and often," he said, as he glanced at the labels outside the parcels, and read, "*Strength for work,*" "*Support in sickness,*" "*Extra comforts for the winter,*" "*Seed for sowing,*" "*Opportunities for service,*" "*Stores for Christmas-keeping,*" "*New Year's gifts,*" with the words written underneath this parcel:

"If ye, being evil, know how to give good gifts unto your children, how much more shall your Father which is in Heaven give good things to them that ask Him!" *

How Adam longed to open that box! Then he saw that it was dated three years before, when he had been so low down—so ill and poor—that he had gone on saying over and over, "Thou hast covered Thyself with a cloud, that my prayer should not pass through." †

"The block was at your own door, Adam, you see," was the grave observation. "That box is of the kind which your Lord uses for His choicest gifts."

"And! why! I *do* declare!" exclaimed Adam, in amaze, "if a shining silvery garment isn't there, hanging up, such as I told Widow Fulljoy might be for her, but couldn't be for one low and poor like me!" And high up above his head sparkled, indeed, a glistening robe made exactly to his size, and bearing the label, "THE GARMENT OF PRAISE."‡

---

* Matthew 7:11

† Lamentations 3:44

‡ Isaiah 61:3

"And *there's* something else!" he said with a sorrowful surprise, "all ready labelled for me in that crystal bottle! How little I knew! 'OIL OF JOY FOR MOURNING!' And more and more! What's that up there? If my eyes don't deceive me, that's the very thing I went moaning and groaning for the want of, till I pretty near wore out every one's patience!" and he pointed to a basket of fairest make, which had once been wreathed round with hearts'-ease and moss, so tenderly that you saw love and planning in every bit, though the flowers had faded and the moss withered. On it were the words, "ABUNDANCE OF PEACE."*

"That's our Lord's own handwriting," said the Messenger, gravely. "You see it was dated in the drought-season years ago."

"My sore time of need!" said Adam; "and I wrote down that day in my private book, *'For peace I had bitterness,'*† because I thought my Lord was displeased and

---

* Psalm 37:11
† Isaiah 38:17

hiding His favors from me; and that He hadn't read my petition."

"But you kept your door shut, Adam; you never went to your Covenant-book and saw that the peace was in your birthright, or remembered that the petition was taken from your Lord's own promise, and that, if He was true, what you had to do was to look out for it as sure as the sun shines, because His Son brought it for you Himself."

"And that lamp up in the corner, and those glasses; they've got my name on them too!" continued Adam, exploring further and further, with a sort of sadness in his voice.

His Guide took them down. "I gave out those glasses for you," he said. "Here is a bit of your own writing tacked on to the parcel!" and he read the words, "*Open Thou mine eyes that I may behold wondrous things out of Thy law!*" *

"Ah! that's what I always put up before I look to my Covenant-book," said Adam; "and I've sometimes longed to understand

---

* Psalm 119:18

more, but have seemed to see so little. My neighbor, now, she's always boasting of her glasses, and sees to read so much that my poor eyes never could make out that it's like a surprise to me all she finds out in her book."

"Did you ever *expect* to get them, or look out for fresh light to be sent to you on your Lord's own word?" asked his Guide. "Why, man, there are promises and promises in that Covenant-book and bank-notes let in to the pages, and revealings of all that your Lord wants to do for you in befriending you, that you never see without His extra light, which I myself prepared for you in this very lamp, and without this second-sight, so to speak, which you, as well as your neighbor, might have had with these glasses, which are called 'Opening of eyes to the blind.' *

"But now it is time to come away. Only remember, Adam, that our Lord is so good and gracious that I am not without a hope that some of these treasures may yet find their way to your cottage, and that when

---

* Psalm 146:8

He passes by and looks at it, it may have ceased to bring such a discredit on His love as it does now."

But, as they passed, a large detached building caught Adam's glance which he had not noticed before.

"May I know the meaning of that fine storehouse?" he asked. "The royal crown is above the entrance, so it must, I gather, be of our Lord's building up."

His Guide turned towards it. "It is a Royal Exchange Office, Adam," he replied. "Many a petition cannot be answered just as poor short-sighted people think best. To get according to their prayers would often be their misery. That place is where our Lord Himself considers these applications and changes His grants to what is really most for their good. Some pray for life here, and they get life forever and ever beyond. Some ask for success and speedy deliverance and they get disappointments which bring them nearer to Him who will deliver them gloriously *in* trouble,* if not always *out*

---

* Job 5:19

of trouble.* Some ask for health of body, and they get health of soul instead, and learn what it is to gain the highest attainable gift of a submitted will, which brings changeless peace, and is worth all the prosperity-gifts put together. Oh, if only people knew all the care that our Lord gives to the exchanges carried on for His own in what is called the *'Commuted Petitions Department,'* they would wonder at His love in caring to do all this for their good with never a failure!"

"And may I yet once more be allowed to ask the name of that more distant store, which has a large and peculiar sort of clock over it, and a sun-dial in front?" said Adam, pointing to a well-sheltered building towards which some empty wagons were being rapidly driven. "Over the gates the inscription looks to me like 'THOUGH IT TARRY, WAIT!' " †

"That," said the Guide, "is the 'DE-LAYED BLESSINGS STORE OFFICE.' Take

---

* Psalm 91:15; Isaiah 33:2
† Habakkuk 2:3

this glass, and you will read underneath the words:

> " 'Therefore will the Lord wait,
> that He may be gracious unto you,
> And therefore will He be exalted,
> that He may have mercy upon you:
> For the Lord is a God of judgment:
> Blessed are all they that wait for Him.' *

"That clock never goes too fast or too slow, and is so constructed that, when the shadow on the dial shows that 'the time of the promise draws nigh,'† it sounds, as an alarum, a warning to the messengers to be ready at once for the delivery of the stored blessings, which, the moment that 'the fulness of the time is come,'‡ are sent forth from the gates. It's not always that the petitioners' doors are found open; for delayed blessings too often come as a surprise even to the Lord's constant remembrancers. When they are still found waiting, and expecting after long tarrying, they receive a

---

* Isaiah 30:18
† Acts 7:17
‡ Galatians 4:4

*'Great is thy faith! be it unto thee even as thou wilt!'** which they are not likely to forget.

"It takes a long time for some pensioners to learn that 'Delays are not denials.' Zacharias would not believe even the angel-messenger who told him the blessing was on its way to his house; and not for many a month was his tongue, tied because of unbelief, loosed to send in the thanksgiving.† When the blessings came to the door of Mary of Jerusalem in the shape of Peter himself, after only a little season of waiting, the very people who had been day and night getting up and sending out petitions for his deliverance would not believe that their Lord had heard them; and while the answer was knocking at the closed gate outside, they cried to the porteress who told its coming, 'Thou art mad!'‡

"The Romans had been petitioning for three years that Paul might come to them; but there were good reasons why the blessing was delayed. A tumult, a hurricane, and a shipwreck were all put in harness to

---

* Matthew 15:28

† Luke 1:5-25, 57-64

‡ Acts 12:1-16

38

bring him to their doors, bound as a prisoner*; but yet their petition that he might have 'a prosperous journey by the will of God, in order that he might impart unto them some spiritual gift,' + was made good as neither he nor they had expected, and in far richer measure for the delay. Onesimus and Philemon were amongst those who found that out.‡

"Ah! there are secrets of love and wisdom in the workings of the 'Delayed Blessings Department' which are little dreamt of!" added the Guide gravely. "Men would pluck their mercies green when their Lord would have them ripe; but if only they knew the preciousness in His sight of the faith that can wait and can trust in the dark, they would understand more of His words: '*Strengthened according to His glorious power unto all patience.§ Wait, I say, on the Lord!*' "**

* These events are chronicled from Acts 21:27 all the way through the end of the book, chapter 28.

† Romans 1:10-11

‡ Philemon 10-19

§ Colossians 1:11

** Psalm 27:14

Then they went back into the sunshine, and, leaving behind them the various buildings connected with the "Missed Blessings Offices," passed once again by the royal storehouses which they had seen at the first. A wagon was being laden in the front court by the servants, who were making ready to start. It seemed to Adam, from the anxious care bestowed, that some very choice packages were being lifted into it, and, to his surprise, the name of his old neighbor was written in full upon one or two which at once met his eyes.

"Is this your afternoon delivery?" asked his Guide.

"It's morning and afternoon and evening to that pensioner," was the answer. "*Expectation Corner*, we call her place! And our Lord Himself sees so much to each package going out to her door, that you'd think He had hardly any one else to care for. Her petitions! why they come up so fast, that if there were any end to these stores, and if there were many more like her, we'd be going bankrupt! But '*Ask, and ye shall receive,'* is the word here; and *'riches in glory'* † don't lessen by giving, and His orders are *'Men ought always to pray and not to faint.'‡* It's seldom we pass Widow Full-joy's door that she isn't waiting for us with a smile and a receipt ready, and with arms stretched out for her gifts, and with *'Bless the Lord, O my soul, and forget not all His benefits!'§* for her psalm of thanks. A good bit of our work down in that part of the estate will be over soon I guess, when the widow's place is empty, and her petitions stop coming in."

"So her call is near at hand?" said Adam's Guide, as he glanced at the parcels directed to her.

"Aye, they do say that our Lord has pretty nigh finished getting ready the rooms in His own palace where she is to live royally with Him, and that all her petitions which she has been sending in these years and years will show out in a deal of the bravery that's been making ready for

---

* Matthew 7:7-8
† Philippians 4:19
‡ Luke 18:1
§ Psalm 103:2

her. She'll not be wanting much more of their ministry, I reckon, who are sent down to minister to the heirs of the Salvation Land!" *

Adam glanced at the labels on one or two of the packages which bore Widow Fulljoy's name. On the first — which seemed like a crystal cup containing some precious cordial—was written, "STRENGTH FOR ENDURANCE," and the words were underneath, *"In the day when thou calledst I answered thee, and strengthened thee with strength in thy soul."*† As was often the custom in the sending out of the parcels from the royal storehouses, the petition, in her own handwriting, which had claimed the gift, was attached to it as a memorandum, and Adam recognized it in a moment, as he read the words: *"I will go in the strength of the Lord God: I will make mention of Thy righteousness, even of Thine only. O God, Thou hast taught me from my youth: and hitherto have I declared Thy wondrous works. Now also when I am old and grey-headed, O God, forsake*

---

* Hebrews 1:14
† Psalm 138:3

me not: until I have showed Thy strength unto this generation, and Thy power to every one that is to come." *

The next parcel was labelled "VIEWS OF THE HEAVENLY CITY AND ITS DELIGHTS." And underneath the label you could read: "*Eye hath not seen, nor ear heard, neither have entered into the heart of man, the things which God hath prepared for them that love Him. But God hath revealed them unto us by His Spirit.*"†

"Ah!" said the Guide, "she will have a rare time with those views—'the evidences of things not seen.'‡ See, there is an autograph note fastened on to the clasp, '*Blessed is she that believed: for there shall be a performance of those things which were told her from the Lord.*' "§

Another gift drew Adam's notice from its peculiar shape, and from the words of the address; for under the widow's name was written, "*Poor of this world; rich in faith;*

---

* Psalm 71:16-18

† I Corinthians 2:9-10

‡ Hebrews 11:1

§ Luke 1:45

and heir of the kingdom." [*] Its form was like that of an Æolian harp[†]; and even as he looked, a breath from his guide on the strings brought forth sounds of such exquisite harmony that they seemed to Adam too ravishing for mortal ear. He fancied that the chords formed themselves into words which sounded like the echo from a distance of a chorus of voices singing, *"Worthy is the Lamb that was slain to receive power, and riches, and wisdom, and strength, and honour, and glory, and blessing."* [‡]

"She is favored," said his guide; " 'the musical instruments of God'[§] are still, as long ago, given out to the chosen among His praising ones. The music and the hymns of the royal palace will be echoed around her to the end, until the messenger choirs come down with the royal chariots to her own door, and chant the bridal song for the Homeward procession: *'Lo, the winter is past, the rain is over and gone: the flowers*

---

[*] James 2:5

[†] A kind of harp wherein strings are stretched over an open box which the wind plays; a *wind harp*.

[‡] Revelation 5:12

[§] I Chronicles 16:42

appear on the earth; the time of the singing of birds is come. My beloved spake, and said unto me, Rise up, my love, my fair one, and come away!" *

Adam quite distinctly read a line or two of the supplication attached to the parcel in accordance with which this gift was sent. "*As the hart panteth after the water brooks, so panteth my soul after Thee, O God. The Lord will command His lovingkindness in the daytime, and in the night His song shall be with me.*"†

But he might not stay longer. His Guide brought him swiftly back to the cottage which he had quitted to learn so much. There it was! poor and sad-looking enough; but the sunlight streamed in at the window as it had not done for many a day. And on the table where he had left it lay Adam's Covenant-book. The wind from the open casement played among its leaves, and, as he and his Guide came back into the room, the words, bathed in sunshine, glittered into sight, "*He that spared not His own*

---

* Song of Solomon 2:11-12, 13

† Psalm 42:1, 8

Son, but delivered Him up for us all, how shall He not with Him also freely give us all things? It is Christ that died, yea, rather that is risen again, Who is even at the right hand of God, Who also maketh intercession for us. Who shall separate us from the love of Christ?' *

Then *"The Lord fulfil all thy petitions!"*† sounded like a strain of music through the room; and, when Adam turned round, his Visitor was gone.

~

I wish you could see Adam Slowman as he now is. You would think that Widow Fulljoy, when the royal carriages came down to take her to the palace, which they did before long, had left him a legacy of songs and praising. You would hear from his open door her favorite words ringing out:

"When long ago I took Thee at Thy word
    My sins were washed away;
  Now for all else I claim Thy promise, Lord,
    As mine for every day!"

---

* Romans 8:32, 34-35
† Psalm 20:5

If you could look into his cottage, you would see tokens of his Lord's love and thought on every shelf and in every corner, and you would hear of the mercy which had forgiven past doubts and misgivings concerning his royal Master's care, while he would tell you of how blessings, which he had long missed, had been graciously granted to him. He would go on joyfully to say how, day by day, he looks out for the King's messengers and welcomes the King's store-wagons. He would tell you of the green pastures and still waters outside, to which he has entrance in right of his tenancy on the Redeemed Land, and of his precious pass-key with "MINE: *thine!*" * graven on the handle—the key which before he had allowed to get so rusty that it would scarcely turn in the locks of the gates admitting to different portions of the royal estates. He would tell you of the rich fruits which grow for him in the enclosed gardens, and of the sacred meetings with his Lord's own messenger, nay, with his Lord

---

* John 17:10; 16:15

Himself; and of how, all through, the same gracious Sovereign has heard his petition, and has remembered for him the covenant, and has made it good to him when he has been too weak, and often too short-sighted, to know all its meaning for himself. All this he would tell you, and much more.

But I must pause.

The thought which has gone into this little story is so clear that its outworking can hardly be called that of an allegory. *"I perish with hunger!"* * is, alas! the cry not always confined to the prodigal son. Are there not many of the Lord's own children who, placing their record of reception beside His charters† of promise, are constrained to ask themselves whether indeed those promises in their fulness and freshness are still in force, whether the promissory notes on the King's storehouses are still honored for the procuring of all that they are set forth as bringing down from His hand?

---

* Luke 15:17

† A *charter* is a document issued by a sovereign conferring certain rights and privileges.

Dear friend, what of our "ships of desire sent out to the land of spices and pearls"?[*] What of our traffic with Heaven? *"My expectation is from Him!"* [†] Is this really our motto, as it is the merchant's awaiting the return of treasure-laden vessels, sent forth empty to the unseen coast? Is our watchword, *"On Thee do I wait all the day"*?[‡]

See how really St. Paul sent out definite petitions, and looked for and received the supplies: *"Having therefore obtained help of God, I continue unto this day."*[§] *"I know that this shall turn to my salvation through your prayers, and the supply of the Spirit of Jesus Christ, according to my earnest expectation, and my hope that in nothing I shall be ashamed."*[**] There is no doubt here as to the line of communication being open between earth and Heaven.

---

[*] Consider I Kings 22:48-49 & II Chronicles 9:21; 20:35-37, the sense of this paragraph being that we ought to look for Heaven's riches as much as we do earth's.

[†] Psalm 62:5

[‡] Psalm 25:5

[§] Acts 26:22

[**] Philippians 1:19-20

It may be that this little book has fallen into the hands of one of the Royal Family of God—of one of His own children, living in the land of Forgiveness of Sin, and yet leading a life of spirit-poverty—of soul penury. Dear friend, are you poor when you want to be rich? Are you mourning over empty vessels, while your Lord longs to pour you out a blessing that there shall not be room enough to receive it? If so, will you think over what is written for you in your own "Covenant-book,"—God's Holy Word of Promise? Remember that no heart petition sent up in the name of Jesus Christ, our Sin-bearer and Intercessor, can lose its way between earth and Heaven. Remember that He is more ready to hear than we to pray. Remember that He still says, "According to your faith be it unto you," * and that if you ask for the faith, He loves and longs to give it.

Shall not we, then, now, take up our stand at "EXPECTATION CORNER" more truly than ever before? Shall not we ask Him to enable us that we may live as

---

* Matthew 9:29

should live the children of the King, show-ing forth His praise who hath made us, unto our God, kings and priests? *

We may be low down, aged, weak in body, slow of speech, stricken with sorrow; but let us remember what stands written for us by one so far down, that from the depths of the sea, he cried, "The depths closed me round about: the weeds were wrapped about my head."† Found he not that even from the ocean bed, there was a path to Heaven, and to the ear of his Father? *When my soul fainted within me, I remembered the Lord, and my prayer came in unto Thee, into Thine Holy Temple.*‡ And found he not also, to his joy, that there was, in like manner, a path for the Lord's mercy and help from the heights of Heaven to the caverns of the sea? And when the deliver-ance came he forgot not the praise: "But I will sacrifice unto Thee with the voice of thanksgiving; I will pay *that* that I have vowed. Salvation *is* of the Lord."§

---

* Revelation 1:6

† Jonah 2:5

‡ Jonah 2:7

§ Jonah 2:9

So for us let the clear psalm note ring out to-day:

"MY SOUL, WAIT ONLY UPON GOD:
MY EXPECTATION IS FROM HIM!"

And may the secret of Heaven, confided to the disciples when their Lord was about to leave them in a cold and dark world, be proved as of ever-fresh assurance by His chosen ones, to whom it has been handed down from generation to generation: *"Ask, and ye shall receive, that your joy may be full!"* *

FIN.

---

* John 16:24

See how this story was written long ago, yet it expresses a major theme in the Church today—that God's people have failed to take hold of His promises (as much as they could anyway). See how we have not ever been barred from taking hold of the promises God made to us—as though somehow our era has easier access to them than those of earlier days, and so if we boast of so little, so must have they. Yet there were some at least who understood that the promises are sovereign charters for the rights and privileges of the people, to live in a manner as befits children of a King.

They were recorded in a Covenant-book for us because God understood our need for a reference. Those so often interpreted as quaint and outdated understood this truth better than many of us do today. How humbling. But how often do we disparage the long-published? Or we wave away some profitable piece of authorship because "I have already read that"? −as though there is no profit to be had in re-reading something. (Or because—in our pride of life—its tone is not as erudite as some other piece of literature.)

We have all believed many lies—not merely historically or reportedly. The father of lies has labored long to effect the seepage of falsehoods into every area of culture. Let us toss all the lies we can identify over our shoulder as so many useless, broken things, and trustingly rely on God to reveal any others as we travel along. Let us look up and look on down this ever soul-drawing Way of Salvation, and ask ourself this: is there something in all those ideologies we tend to cling to that is really of greater value than what God offers us in replacement? For remember— He never takes away without blessing with something better. This is, in truth, why He takes away, so that our vessel being emptied, it can be filled again, and with what is better.

God bless you richly.

NOTE on the term *anchorite*: in simple terms, an anchorite lives largely in seclusion for the sake of the well-being of Christ's Church. Days center around prayer, the elimination of distractions (in elder days this was known as asceticism), and serious consecration to a calling that requires them to be of service to others, particularly spiritual service — i.e., the kind of service that does not interfere with living an intense Christ-centered life. Historically they were often women who had retired from community life (for instance after being widowed) and who had resources to share with the Church; but let us not be limited by old applications of long-held definitions. Any true God-given calling is liberating, not confining (though at times the soul can feel the burden of it).

Hear the word of Hebrews 6:17-20 — "Wherein God, willing more abundantly to shew unto the heirs of promise the immutability of His counsel, confirmed it by an oath: that by two immutable things, in which it was impossible for God to lie, we might have a strong consolation, who have fled for refuge to lay hold upon the hope set before us: which hope we have as an anchor of the soul, both sure and stedfast, and which entereth into that within the vail; whither the forerunner is for us entered, even Jesus, made an high priest for ever after the order of Melchisedec."

In short, having laid hold of the Anchor which is Christ, some are called to become spiritual anchors for the stability of His Body. Anchorites follow Jesus our Lord as He fulfills His calling as our High Priest. They serve in His Temple all their days, as Anna did (Luke 2:36-37).

These epistles are a result of that labor.

If you have time, please visit littleanchorsofthechurch.net.

Milton Keynes UK
Ingram Content Group UK Ltd.
UKHW032051201124
451474UK00005B/285

9 798330 541652